Make Your Own Dancing Slime

Julia Garstecki and Stephanie Derkovitz

BLACK
RABBIT
BOOKS

Hi Jinx is published by Black Rabbit Books
P.O. Box 3263, Mankato, Minnesota, 56002.
www.blackrabbitbooks.com
Copyright © 2020 Black Rabbit Books

Marysa Storm, editor; Michael Sellner, designer;
Omay Ayres, photo researcher

Names: Garstecki, Julia, author. | Derkovitz, Stephanie, author.
Title: Make your own dancing slime : by Julia Garstecki and
Stephanie Derkovitz.
Description: Mankato, Minnesota : Black Rabbit Books, [2020] |
Series: Hi jinx. Make your own fun | Includes bibliographical references
and index. | Audience: Ages 9-12. | Audience: Grades 4 to 6.
Identifiers: LCCN 2018034734 (print) | LCCN 2018037241 (ebook) |
ISBN 9781680729399 (e-book) | ISBN 9781680729337 (library binding) |
ISBN 9781644660645 (paperback)
Subjects: LCSH: Handicraft–Juvenile literature. | Gums and resins,
Synthetic–Juvenile literature. | Toys–Juvenile literature.
Classification: LCC TT297 (ebook) | LCC TT297 .F45 2016 (print) |
DDC 745.5–dc23
LC record available at https://lccn.loc.gov/2018034734

Printed in China. 1/19

Image Credits

Black Rabbit Books: Michael Sellner, 7 (bowl, speaker, cables), 8 (bowls), 11
(bowl), 12 (bowl), 14 (btm circle), 15 (speaker), 16, 16–17 (speaker), 19 (speaker);
Shutterstock: Arcady, 7 (sticky note); brux, 16–17 (headphones); BW Folsom, 7
(straw); Danny Smythe, 8 (water); Denis Cristo, 11 (girl); Elizabeth A.Cummings, 7
(food coloring); Feaspb, Cover (slime), 4–5 (slime), 14–15 (slime); ffolas, 8 (starch),
12 (starch); gn8, 16–17 (bkgd); Galyna G, 19 (bkgd); GraphicsRF, Cover (left
monster), 3 (monster), 4 (left monster), 16–17 (monsters), 21 (monsters); HitToon,
10 (drops); jarabee123, 2–3, 12 (slime), 20 (slime); kiri11, 7 (plastic); Mark Herreid,
7 (cups), 8 (cups), 12 (cup); Mega Pixel, 7 (tape); mohinimurti, Back Cover (blgd),
4 (bkgd), 15 (bkgd); NIRUT RUPKHAM, 7 (phone); onair, 7 (fork), 11 (fork);
opicobello, 10 (tear); Pasko Maksim, Back Cover (top), 13 (tear), 17, 23 (top),
24; pitju, 6 (page curl), 10 (page curl), 18, 21 (page curl); pixfly, 14 (top circle);
Ron Dale, 5, 6 (marker stroke), 13 (marker stroke), 15 (marker stroke), 17
(marker stroke), 20 (marker stroke); Ron Leishman, 6 (girl, table), 18–19
(boy, straw), 23 (btm); Slava_kovtun, 8 (hand), 12 (hand, fork);
TAW4, 1; Teguh Mujiono, Cover (right monster), 4 (right
monster); y Rvector, Cover (speaker, music notes), 4
(speaker, music notes), 16–17 (music notes)
Every effort has been made to contact copyright
holders for material reproduced in
this book. Any omissions will be
rectified in subsequent
printings if notice is given
to the publisher.

Contents

Chapter 1
Get Ready for
Some Fun!

Making your own fun is easy! It can also be super slimy. That's right! Just keep reading to learn how to make your own dancing slime. Dancing slime is a special **substance** that moves to music with heavy base. Whip some up for a groovin' good time.

Chapter 2
Let's Make!

It doesn't take much to make dancing slime. You only need a few simple ingredients. Once it's made, you'll just need to prepare the dance floor. Then you'll be jamming in no time.

What You'll Need

1 cup (240 milliliters) cornstarch

½ cup (120 ml) water

medium mixing bowl

liquid food coloring (optional)

straw

plastic wrap

device that plays music

masking tape

fork

subwoofer speaker

stereo/audio adapter cables

a **responsible** adult to help you

Make the Slime

1 Pour the water into the bowl.

2 Add just ½ cup (120 ml) of cornstarch to the water.

3 Use the fork to mix the water and cornstarch together. Stir until the mixture is smooth.

4 If you want colored slime, add a drop of food coloring. Mix well.

5 Repeat Step 4 until you've added about five drops of food coloring.

6 Add the rest of the cornstarch to the bowl. Stir the mixture while you add the cornstarch.

7 Mix until the cornstarch and water are combined. The mixture will act like a solid once it's all mixed.

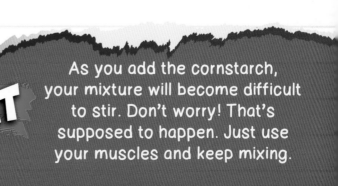

HINT As you add the cornstarch, your mixture will become difficult to stir. Don't worry! That's supposed to happen. Just use your muscles and keep mixing.

Prepare the Dance Floor

1 Plug in your speaker, and turn it on. Be sure the volume is low to start.

2 Plug the device you'll play music with into the speaker. Be sure it's on and the volume is low to start.

3 Pick the right song. You'll want to choose a song with heavy base. **Dubstep** is a good choice.

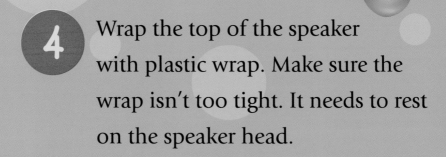

4 Wrap the top of the speaker with plastic wrap. Make sure the wrap isn't too tight. It needs to rest on the speaker head.

5 **Secure** the plastic wrap with tape.

HINT Wait until the slime is on the dance floor to play your music.

Start Dancing

1 Pour some slime into the covered speaker cone. Be sure not to overfill the cone. The slime shouldn't spill over the sides.

2 Start playing the music.

3 Turn up the music to get your slime dancing.

17

Helping Your Slime Dance

Don't worry if your slime sits out the first few dances. It can take time to find the perfect song. Your slime might need some **encouragement** to start dancing too. All you need to do is grab a straw. Then blow air through it onto the slime while music plays. The air should get your slime moving.

19

Chapter 3
Get in on the
Hi Jinx

Slime can do more than just dance. Some slime can make farting noises. Other types of slime are used for special effects in movies. Many plastic objects, such as small toys, are made with slimy materials. The slime is placed in **molds** and hardened into shapes. Slime has many uses. Who knows what you might do with slime someday?

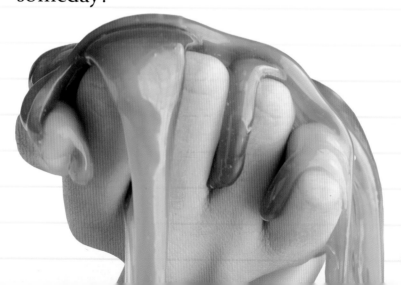

Take It One Step More

1. Blowing air onto the slime will help it start dancing. Why do you think that is?

2. Test out different tunes. What music makes your slime dance the best?

3. This recipe calls for twice as much cornstarch as water. Why do you think the recipe needs so much?

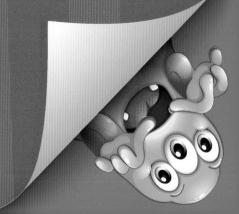

GLOSSARY

device (dee-VIS)—an object, machine, or piece of equipment made for a specific purpose

dubstep (DUHB-step)—a type of electronic dance music having prominent bass lines and syncopated drum patterns

encouragement (en-KUR-ij-muhnt)— something that makes someone more likely to do something

mold (MOHLD)—a hollow form in which something is shaped

responsible (ri-SPON-suh-buhl)— able to be trusted to do what is right or to do things that are expected or required

secure (suh-KEYR)—to hold fast

substance (SUB-stanse)—a physical material from which something is made

BOOKS

Crane, Cody. *Amazing Makerspace DIY Slippery Slime.* A True Book. New York: Children's Press, an imprint of Scholastic, Inc., 2018.

Garstecki, Julia. *Make Your Own Farting Goo.* The Disgusting Crafter. Mankato, MN: Black Rabbit Books, 2019.

Lawrence, Ellen. *Creeping Slime: Slime Molds.* Slime-inators & Other Slippery Tricksters. New York: Bearport Publishing, 2019.

WEBSITES

Dancing Oobleck
www.housingaforest.com/dancing-oobleck/

Dancing Oobleck - Maker Camp
**makercamp.com/projects/
dancing-oobleck**

Parent Craft Projects
www.elmers.com/slime

Don't be afraid to ask your adult for help. Some steps can be tricky.

Mix different colors of food coloring together to create new colors.

The slime might splatter a bit when it dances. It might hit you or your surroundings. Wear old clothes. Make sure you're dancing somewhere that's easy to clean too!